The Artist's Disease

Damien Pragnell

chipmunkapublishing

the mental health publisher

Published by

Chipmunkapublishing

PO Box 6872

Brentwood

Essex CM13 1ZT

United Kingdom

http://www.chipmunkapublishing.com

Chipmunkapublishing gratefully acknowledge the support of Arts Council England.

Author Biography

Damien was born in Seven Hills, Sydney, Australia in 1958. He was one of five children, all of whom are creative. His father was a British Paratrooper and Mentor to Damien. His mother was a warm, supportive woman with her own artistic gifts. When they found out that Damien had bipolar she danced him around the kitchen saying "son, you have the artist's disease'.

Damien has completed qualifications in library studies which compliments his life long love affair with poetry and writing. Damien has also had a long history of involvement with music, theatre and literature. He names his diverse influences as the Beat Poets, Native American Shamanic writings, Pink Floyd, Steve Vai and Vangelis just to name a few. Despite these numerous influences, Damien's voice emerges as a highly original and gifted poet. Damien has entered the chaos and pain of illness and emerged into recovery as a strong, expressive, generous and giving man.

He credits his recovery and positive outlook to family, his writing, a commitment to wellness and the positive supports of the people around him.

Damien Pragnell

Before My Time

Before my time has come and gone.
I want to pen an anthem.
Something bittersweet, yet strong.
The kind that has the D.Js
Raving all day long.

As sure as men are born,
of good intent.
As sure as women can convince you,
they are Heaven sent.
My song will have its roots in blues.
A hook that eases worried heads.

There was a time when my mind was lost,
on the Sixties form of treason.
This time that swells within,
now offers me true freedom.

When my time has come and gone.
A shadow moves across my lifeless form.
Revelation of the Great Beyond.

An angel will surely sing,
my one and only song.
Revealing aspects of the spirit world.
When my time has come and gone.

Like Peas In A Pod

So, if there is no God
No angels up above
We can all still love each other
Just like peas in one large human pod
(I stole that thought from
"Invasion of the Body Snatchers.")

And when we are finished
Weary with these tired old bodies.
Maybe there will be a friend, of which one can give
a nod,
Who will rake the leaves
Off our crumbling bones beneath,
Or every now and then …
turn the rich and fertile sod.

The Artist's Disease

Velvet Hammer

NOTE: (A Hollywood Actor once stated the Director
of the current film he was working on was
prescribed the medication LITHIUM. Known in
Hollywood circles as THE VELVET HAMMER.

Steve Biko, Martin Luther
Not forgetting The Mahatma.
They never raised a fist in anger.
Their love inside A Velvet Hammer.

Florence Nightingale, Mother Theresa
All they wanted was to heal ya!
Charlie Chaplin's brilliant humour
Encompassed in "The Great Dictator"
The roar of such a little man
Knocked the stuffing out of Adolph Hitler.

Marlon Brando and James Dean
The course of drama changed forever,
Neither happy with their lot,
Captured inside grainy celluloid
Carrying "THE METHOD BANNER".

Stanley Kubrick and Ken Russell,
Filming "A Clockwork Orange" and "The Devils"
Whetting our appetites with stunning images
Of mindless violence.

Then there is the way we treat each other.
Father, Mother, Sisters, Brothers.
A braver person walks away

Leaving enemies confused and flustered.

Trying to clog the system with a spanner?
When all it takes is love...
Wrapped inside A Velvet Hammer.

These Feelings Trapped Inside

One day these feelings, trapped deep inside.
Air, water, earth and fire.
This world a woe begotten place,
So few of us survive.

Faith and hope alone
Will not set us free.
We strive to separate,
Right from wrong
Our ever changing destinies.

These feelings that surely hinder us.
Our rage and dissipated souls.
Each in turn will tell our stories
No longer quest forEldorado's Gold.

Runic Cross

Seven stones of mystery.
Form a Runic Cross.
A Karmic riddle solved.
Revealing the path of destiny.
All your future gain.
All your future loss.

A ritual from an Icelandic tower.
Performing upon the witching hour.
Odin's Messengers descend.
Their work that never ends.

The Runic Cross.
For those who seek
The Norsemen's power.
Seven stones of mystery
The future and the past unlocked.

Dream Catcher

A prize possession
Symbol of an Ancient Lore
Created by a once proud tribe
Even the very god's adored.

Did you bring your warriors a deep sound sleep?
Quieten the restless spirit,
Just like the smoke that rose from a pipe of peace.

Keep my nightly visions true
You web and feathered mystery
Fashioned in a hoop
Give meaning to my quest
My nightmare never knew.

Did you bring the stars around your people
Revelling in their childlike dreams.

As I lay upon my bed this night
Let the spirits of your fiercest braves
The wisdom of a Shamans ways
The demons and their evil ways
Dissolved within the morning light.

The Gentle Rains

Where the gentle rains fall nightly.
That's where good farmers want to settle.
Their lives a mix of joy and sorrow,
A rose amongst the stinging nettle.

A love of evil drives certain men,
Beyond the realms of human beings.
The cry for retribution deafening.
The bloodlust never settled.

Where the road to heaven seems never ending.
Where howling dogs lead us to eternal fire.
In the guise of those who know what's best.
While filling their own pockets.

The ocean cannot wash away the blood
Of generations past.

Only God's own lenience can lead us from
damnation.

Where a child waits for recognition.
For a song so sweetly sung.
A new kid on the block stands lonely,
Trying to blend in.

Where all the stars in heaven shimmer,
On a calming summers eve,
For those who search for heavenly answers,
In a world soon cast asunder.

The Artist's Disease

This New Jersey Balladeer
(Bruce Springsteen We Love You)

12/08/2004
Born to breathe in the urban fire.
Dancing out of a West Side Story.
A night flight across the Hudson River.
This New Jersey Balladeer.

Signed his life away,
A faulty record contract,
On the hood of a Chevrolet.
The years that rolled on by
Without a word or a song.

We saw the future of rock and roll,
An angel of the streets,
running wild.
The "E" Street Band never sounded better,
One man's vision of the urban grind.

Growing up a little wiser,
Still yearning for that human touch.
The city of angels holds the key,
His denim jeans and leather jacket
A New York Rhapsody.

The applause of one hundred thousand
Screaming teenage fans,
Soon disappears,
The ghosts of John Steinbeck and
Jack Kerouac whispering their hymns to the open
road,

A world of hurt in each refrain.

The Boss, alone once more
Treads the rain soaked pier,
To have his fortune read by
Madam Maria,
This New Jersey Balladeer
We love you …

Bruce Springsteen

When Push Comes To Shove

When push comes to shove
They'll be no hatred
They'll be no love.
And as Mister Lennon sang
They'll be no hell where we will burn
And no mysteries up above.

All we know.
And all we have, here on planet earth
Trampled into cosmic dust.
When push comes to shove…

Once a nation had twin buildings.
A symbol of their ingenuity.
Crumbling to the ground
This nation lost it's trust
And this is what the future holds
When push comes to shove.

There's a woman
I don't know her name.
One day I know she will call
And I will make her mine.
For this is how good Karma grows
When push comes to shove.

Love Letter

Will she ever understand me.
The way I act when I'm around her.
Can there ever be a future,
With the one I swear I've found.

Time is of the essence.
Or so it seems to me.
Her beauty never alters,
I'm in love with her, you see.

I look for something about her.
The search goes on,
Never falters.
It's captured in her smile,
Her ever present laughter.

My crude jokes don't impress her.
I am so blind to all her needs.
It's there in every woman's eyes,
In all they say, all that they believe.

The Stranger

In his denim shirt and faded jeans.
Across his back a blanket rolled.
And neatly tied the stranger finds his stride.

Maybe sailing wild, veracious seas.
Climbing ancient pyramid's.
Riding camels in Dubai.
Dredging sand or pumping gasoline.
Freedom carries it's own price.

One rule in life to see him through.
Don't look for strife, don't back away.
Through the crowd he makes his way.
A knowing smile upon his face.

A visionary without a sign.
An adventurer whose lost his way.
For one brief moment the tourist
strip has come alive.

Sitting on my coffee break I watched
this comic scene unfold.
The stranger shook hands with every
passer-by then disappeared into the
milling throng.

Would he sleep beneath the stars that night.
Slip away come morning light on a clipper
Bound for China, some new adventure
underway?

The years have passed on by since the stranger
strode through town.
Sometimes I try a reckless grin in his freewheeling,
rambling style.

Could I abandon all to circumstance or take the
Northstar as my guide?
Would the world accept another stranger on
a never-ending high?

The Artist's Disease

Ready For Hiawatha

Ready for hire Watha,
stood outside his tee pee.
Leslie, his girlfriend was not with him.
They had gone their separate ways.

Watha had his CD's, his books and videos.
To last him all his days.

The tribe he lived with hunted,
fished and gathered berries and sweet corn.
Yet Watha had grown tired of this,
he wanted so much more.

At night the ceremonies
bought the tribes together.
Tunkashila, The Great Spirit, offered a pipe
of peace,
so all could share his love.

Inside the Shamans lodge.
The walls adored with skins and bones.
Watha sat before this magic man,
Listened while he spoke.

"Watha, you must undertake a quest."
"Travel to the white mans city.
Find out why they act this way.
There you'll find yourself."

Gathering on the river bank.
The tribe said their goodbyes.

They presented Watha with some gifts.
A dark suit, shirt collar and a tie.
A suitable disguise.

In time Watha found the city.
A cold and soulless place.
He longed to go back home,
was this the reason for his quest?

Ready for hire Watha.
Found nothing that he liked.
Would he decide to leave the city life,
once again, become a child of paradise.

Only Tunkashila, The Great Spirit,
knew the answer, to this question,
but he would not be saying yet.

When Men Sing

When men sing
The Heavens rock.
A stomping ground
for mankind's soulful blues.

When men dance
from Nijinsky to Baryshnikov,
they are the lords of self expression
in soft kid leather shoes.

When men romance
their hearts desire,
the Heavens sigh.
For just a moment the earth is balanced.

When men wage war.
The songs degraded and deranged.
The dancer stops to march in line,
the romance lost on widow's faces.

When men take a stand
for all they believe in.
They sing, they dance, love and fight,
without a whimper, but a mighty roar.

A short Lived Introspection

I do not know what's wrong with me.
A life of unfulfilled destinies.
The declarations, infatuations
the torches carried high.

The questions as always,
Unanswered,
the soul unsatisfied.

Then again,
by sleight of hand
I could cover all my mislaid plans,
embellished long forgotten stories.
The mind so filled with fantasy.

The answer to the questions,
so easy just to live a lie.
Harder though to swallow unearned pride.

Reluctant Phoenix

I shall not rise, a phoenix
when the spirit has burned low
nor take up causes for rewards
leaving nothing left to show.

On summer days devoid of rain
a gentle breeze will flow
the days will follow night I pray
for as long as we can know.

I shall not breathe in cold grey ashes
Ascend to heaven borne on fiery wings.

No, a gust of air that makes you sigh
a breeze upon a lapping tide.
This will be my eternity, my longing,
my tomorrow.

The Question

Who will give me dignity
if I do not grasp the nettle.
Who will grant me liberty
if I do not fight the battle.

Who will recall my childhood.
Those who played a part?
Who will test my feelings,
give me a change of heart.

And who will gather at my bedside
when I've done all that I can.
Who will say a heartfelt prayer,
then send me on my way.

These questions linger on the air,
For the answers I must wait.

Who will laugh out loud
at life's absurdities.
Who wants to walk the path alone,
not me, my friends, not me.

The Days Unwind

The days unwind
A minute here, a moment there.
Unfurling hopes and childhood dreams
The tender nights that lovers share.

The days are kind
To those that care,
A vision in a fertile mind
A world that's large enough to share.

The days define
The time spent here.
Rolling into Autumn years
An end to all the pain and fear.

The days are mine as well as yours
Perhaps we can meet up halfway there,
United in a common cause.

The days unwind like slender threads.

Time gone is really absolute.
The hours and minutes slowly burn
The ashes that we live to mourn

Of days that will not be returned.

The Ghosts of Morning

As we exorcise the ghosts of morning
we hope blind ambition will not corrupt us.
Nor our ego's fail to blame us
for each others selfish ways.

In these days of striving forward,
cannot help look back on our childhoods.
A time when truth was just an option,
today it struggles to survive.

The spell of morning broken
An argument intruding,
on once peaceful family settings,
spilt by anger soon forgotten.

The ghosts of mornings soon return
as spectral thoughts return to haunt us,
exposed upon our sunlight windows
we give thanks they did not claim us.

One Man's Trash

One man's trash.
His woman's displeasure,
all his eggs in one basket,
to be played with at his leisure.

One man's steel garage.
His seat of power
To find the solace that he seeks.
Where he can wile away the hours.

One man's religion
that gives him strength.
When life turns sour.
Someone to meet him up above,
when the clock strikes his final hour.

One man's trash.
His junk pile made to order.
Rich men shake their heads,
yet their wealth is not much better.

"Cause we will enter paradise.
All joining hands,
dressed in the altogether.

A short Delivery

Deliver me from judgment.
I, the eternal optimist,
content to take the middle road
turning grey skies into blue.

Offer me redemption.
Someone else must pay the cost.
Eternal lovers light the flame,
gathering the legions of the lost.

Examine my intentions.
The powers that govern all.
See if they ring true,
keep the world enthralled.

Deny me living hatred.
The fires that sear the flesh.
The tongues that spit the fiercest words,
deliver me from madmen's songs.

The Artist's Disease

Chuckle on!

What can put a smile,
On all the different colours
On all the separate races?

Happiness within, awaiting to be born.
Gazing round the world
One word springs to mind
Sums up the local tribes
Simply put ... forlorn.

The news at night is rarely warm and rosy,
the battle rages on between those that love and
those that hate.
Getting hard to just ... relate.

The laughter of the world.
Reasons seemingly poor cousin.
Worth more than wealth and winning awards
Our universe is really small.
Too fragile to keep points and scores.

What price can you put on a smile?
It costs so little, yet never goes unnoticed.
It's just what our creator ordered
Chuckle on...

Let's make it our religion.
A high rolling revolution.

Could It Be

Could it be more than mere coincidence.
A host of unrelated accidents.
As we are moving ever closer
to the end we know, inevitable.

Staring from the open window.
The birds and trees in perfect union.
The sun retires to rise again
Only for a moment, my friends.

The deeds and games of earth bound angels.
As people rush to claim the credit.
Could this be a grand illusion
Or a life beginning as it travels

An endless journey through…
Eternity.

The Mentor and the Protégé

The Mentor and the Protégé
The meetings, the desire to teach
life's mysteries.
Soaked up like a sponge.
So many paths, so much knowledge to impart.

Endless days, discussions, impressions.
Male or female, it makes no difference.
Elderly or child, the joy of learning awakening.
The spell is only broken,
when the boundaries are crossed.
The mentor hears the hollow ring of one,
no longer listening.
The protégé is alone once more,
to unravel what was learned.

Another meeting dawns.
The wisest of the pair
never stated, never clear.
Separating the brightness from the darkness.
The joy of learning, awakened, defined.

The spell is only broken.
On the crossing of the boundaries.

The Knowledge

The search for one perfect life.
The product of inquiring minds.
Everything we do or say,
catalogued upstairs,
bound to come in handy…
Some day.

Endless hours, the midnight oil.
Knowing everything that happened yesterday,
won't protect you from the world…
Today.

Whether you remember,
the facts and figures taught and learned.
Your speech rolls off a silken tongue.
The answers to the universal questions,
always close at hand.

It's only useful if it does some good.
Makes life for you and yours worthwhile.
No, no one likes a smartass,
lets pretend we don't like fooling round.

Knowledge…

The guiding light of kings and scholars,
the Kryptonite of fools.

The Artist's Disease

In the Bare Light

To be able to see life as it happens,
the beginnings, the middle and the end.
Yet have no relations, no partners
not even one good friend.

To dance in the bare light.
Inside Nijinsky's shadow
then create a dance that's new.

To build a bomb that could destroy the world.
Makes you think, doesn't it.

Master's of reality.
Illusion too.
Never knowing peace of mind
never anything to do.

Acute perception.
A passionate intensity.
Answers hard to find.
A single friend to say …"hello."

No one knows what messages they send.
The beginning, the middle and the end.

To dance in the bare light.
The beginning, the middle and the end.
To move out of Nijinsky's shadow.
The genius to create a dance that's new.

To home in on one aspect of performance

Walk the tightrope between genius and insanity.
The roar of devoted crowds.
A catharsis for the raging spirit,
Set free, set free.

Hired Guns

From my time of realization
I learnt all the fiery legends.
Heroic stories of bloody battles won.
Never questioning the outcome,
until the doubts began to plague my mind.

Were they really a nation's daughters and sons.
Battle hardened killers or simply hired guns.

Then I realized how it was.
They were there. That's how it was.
Now daily living with their pasts.
Talking, writing in a secret language,
to blood brothers, to surviving mates.
Six years sleeping on the cold night earth.
What bed do they make now?
What recollections haunt their midnight hours?
A surreal vision of hell.

And I will shut my mouth on this.
Keep my opinions to myself.
They were not a nation's daughters and sons.
Hardened killers or even hired guns.

They were simply young men and women.
Allowing us to live our lives.

One Man's Weakness

Several million years ago
we had struck stone upon stone
suddenly we had fire for warmth,
we had ascended nature's throne.
On that dreamtime morning
When we had learnt to stand,
When even angels sang
every beast that trod or flew or even swam,
learned to fear our cruelty,
this vengeful beast called … man!

Several million years ago
a golden dawn descended
on the virgin valleys and plains.
Man stood in wide eyed wonder,
"was it I who created divinity
or was it there when time began?"

And so we've come full circle,
Our once great paradise slowly turns to slime.
Our oceans reek of spilt oil and uranium,
Another man placed in isolation
Left wondering.

"Where on earth did I go wrong!"

We covered up our nakedness
to hide our guilt and shame.
Wage war against the differences in each other
in a long forgotten name.
Hopelessly deceived that we are all born

The Artist's Disease

just the same,
as we race towards oblivion,
because one man's weakness is perceived,
in all it's bleakness
as one another's ... gain!

A Seasons Promise

The bleakness of winter's spurning
gives way to spring times yearnings.
Earth mother's ceaseless greening
sounds the death knell to nights foreboding.

The church tower bells are peeling,
celebrating one more Sabbath,
the congregation in one voice singing,
drowning out Satan's laughter.

The ocean lashing the surfing brave,
searching for the ultimate wave.
Two lovers cuddle on the shore,
the northern breeze cannot dampen their ardour
A Sunday picnic followed by a midday slumber.
A long train ride back into the suburbs.
For those of us, lucky enough,
a promise of an endless summer.

Hero For A Minute
A Plea by Damien Pragnell

Can I become a hero,
just for a moment or two.
Bring a crowd of thousands to their feet,
win a Nobel Prize
for preaching global peace.

Will I ever find that special someone
leave this rat race far behind.
Travel with my loving sister once again.
Down the Yellow Brick Road.

Maybe we can all join hands.
Our enemies wait for us to make
the very first move.
Flying closer to the sun
comes to those who face the truth.

Are those teardrops forming
as I write these words and thoughts
on what is now
and where our future lives can lie.

With all the latest in technology
thinking out too loud
following your hearts desire
can sometimes brand you as a trouble maker
an open and shut case
rebellious youth gone wild.

Damien Pragnell

When Storm Clouds Brew

When your down
when storm clouds brew,
gathering around you,
when so called friends cannot reveal
a simple homespun truth.

There is a voice
A glimmer in a sunless sky
Yet this is not the voice that troubles you
From now until you die.

No my friends there is something more
that thrives on honesty and decent life.
A love on the horizon
that waits to be your guide.

This voice does not care
what shape you are
or the riches you have earned
it's always there when you're in need
it is in fact …
                yourself.

When your enemies are through
treating you as a clown
and vengeance seems the only wage for
the sins you swallowed down.

I'm not asking you to turn the other cheek
no, these bastards don't care for love.
just rise above the urban grime,

The Artist's Disease

find yourself some peace mind,
it's there for the taking,
in your parents loving eyes.

When you feel you've lost your youth,
On things no longer clear.
When that storm brews overhead.
Just stand your ground,
embrace the fear, swallow the tears,
this is where the real life begins,
this is where you'll find yourself.

The biggest battle lies within
where storm clouds brew …
                                        inside.

Damien Pragnell

It's All Down Hill From Here

8/05/2005

Not long ago I would spring from bed
the moment the cock crowed.
Now it's a struggle just to rise and shine.
Part my hair to hide the bald spot,
pop in my dentures.

It's all downhill, from here.

Used to stride with confidence,
a suntanned god at least.
Let the beach girls check me out.
Now I'm old enough to be their grandfather.
My smile turned to sardonic leer.

It's all downhill, from here.

Maybe soon I"ll ditch this gig.
Give up the notion of a steady job.
Get married, have some kids
or perhaps I'll return
To the streets I knew so well.
Once more across the rickety wooden bridge.
The hometown crowd cheers.
These dreams embellished with too many beers
wandering off these rusted tracks.
A dollar a page, the writing hack.

It's all downhill, from here.

The Artist's Disease

When Night Eclipses Day

Not content to smell the roses
still wake to find a different way.
Not lying still to feed the worms.
When night eclipses day.

My rebellion fueled by riding laughter,
nameless wonders, morbid clowns.
An idea slowly growing old,
still driven by a wall of sound.

What have I learnt?
These days soon pass.
The, soul ignites and quickly burns,
won't even know when I've had enough.

Pay no attention to my discontent.
Life's fire burns and knows no age.
One day I'll stop and smell the roses
when night eclipses day.

A Mothers Voice

A mothers voice calms a new born babe.
Keeps the beasts and monsters,
the shadows all at bay.

A mothers voice can help her children,
endure the devils rain.
Her legacy a blend of courage, of fire,
love and grace.
Be a fighter, a writer, an actor, a priest.
A king on high down to the least.
A mothers heart can't tell the difference,
yet breaks so easily.

Somewhere I have read, imagined,
that Wellington at Waterloo.
Took orders from his dear departed.
How could he rightly lose.

For those of us who long to see.
Her face aglow from worlds unknown.

For those who share their household still.
Even when they travel on,
the wisdom will remain as now.
The fierce pride of a lioness
keeping beasts and monsters down.

Soaking Up America

Here we live in Paradise.
Rolling aqua waves, golden desert sands.
Born and bred to die right here, my heart
and mind embrace another land.

Just soaking up America.
Dreams of Old World U.S.A.
Plugged into their MTV wearing Homer Simpson's
BVD's.

Call me a traitor if you will,
the eagle and the lonesome dove are waiting
for me there.

Checking out the babes,
strolling Venice Beach.
Frank Zappa's married poodles,
shoot some rounds from Eastward's 45.
Visit New York galleries and view
Warhol's cans of soup.

My nation born on convict stock.
An island growing deep and wide.
A land we struggle to recognize,
when stars and stripes hammers its way home.

Just soaking up America.
Dreams of good old U.S.A,
videos and coke machines,
Wyoming's pastures green.

Damien Pragnell

Just soaking up America,
friends to make and politicians.
In my heart I'll stay here forever more.
Even with those dreams.
The endless silver screen on Hollywood and Vine.

Hate To Be A Hermit

I'd hate to be a hermit,
although I'm almost there.
No-one comes a visiting,
the phone, it never rings.

Don't want to wear a sheepskin,
Grow my beard down to my knees.
Eat locusts, wild honey
to keep myself alive.
(Honey gives me hives.)

Of course I'd need some creature comforts.
CDs, videos, a fridge that's bursting at the seams.
Daily visits from my fellow hermit neighbours,
all the beer that I can drink.

I'd hate the daily contemplation
of my navel full of lint.
In between the hunt for dinner,
field mice and skinks.

That's all for now
the hermit from next door
wants to discuss the state of our sad world.

I'd hate to be a hermit.
But, in a way that's what we are.
Our deepest thoughts and feelings hidden
as we wave to neighbours from afar.

Damien Pragnell

Tails and Whiskers

We shared a special kind of love.
You were black, I was white.
I'd come home and throw my
school bag across the floor.
You, excited to see me
always wanting more.
You knew I had some gifts
A piece of cheese, some rolled oats.
I'd look into your cobalt eyes.
See the innocents and trust.

Then, you became pregnant.
To that surfie type rodent
next door.
How could I afford a family.
Things just wouldn't be the same.

The day you left, I knew we
wouldn't meet again.
A schoolboy friend, Ken,
would care for you.

I brought your favourites
Glazed cherries and raisins.
Your wheel was packed,
your empty toilet roll
which doubled as a bed.
You washed your face
and climbed my hand
to show we'd always be friends.

The Artist's Disease

You had your babies.
They were pink, naked,
Deaf, dumb and blind.
How you loved them just the same.   (all in kind.)

And there you were,
Staring through the wire
of Ken's spacious cage.
as if to say, accusingly,

"Love is not a crime."

Model Citizen

He's a model citizen.
Does not care for criticism.
After work, gathered round the bar.
Of the Hotel "Lucky Star."
He dazzles his work colleagues
with his wit and ripping yarns.

He is a model citizen.
You never catch him bitchin'
about the way his bosses treat him … the ladies,
Well they cannot get enough.

He's still searching for Miss Right.
Til then he takes the pretty ones home each night.
His name is not splashed across the morning
papers.
He's very discreet and ever so polite.

He lives in a modern idiom.
Dresses really smart.
Never wakes up with bad breath.
He does not ever fart.
He's a model citizen.
One day he'll run for President
a force to be reckoned with.
From the tip of his gelled hair
To his camel hair loafers.

He's a model citizen.
You will always find him smiling.
He's just a bag of solid saccharin.

Dead At The Wheel

Whitey was found one morning
dead at the wheel.
Some say he drove too fast,
other cell mates said he had to leave,
he'd eaten all the others cheese.

His mates held a little service,
then buried him in fresh sawdust,
behind the water bottle.\

Whitey was not liked by many,
on this they all agreed,
he drove too fast,
he was always cutting in,
on someone else's turn.

Whitey paid the ultimate price
for being so hard nosed.
His cellmates all gave up a turn
as a mark of respect for the fallen.
Life is hard in a pet shop,
Especially for rodents.

Whitey paid the ultimate price,
But he always broke the rules.

That night, when the owners had gone home.
The cellmates held a little wake.
They turned the wheel at half speed,
they ate some smoked Dutch Edam
and for those who could afford it

some expensive Blue Vein cheese.

All The Same To Me

We all deal with grief
in our own separate ways.
We all live here for a little while,
yet, none of us can stay.

We all have a vision,
of a heaven or a hell.
We all have a mission
although what it is never made quite clear.

We all turn back the years.
Relive those painful memories.
We all have so much passion,
our laughter mixed with tears.

We all have guardian angels
To help us face our fears.
We all succumb to demons,
creating such obsessions,
sometimes our phobias seem so real.

We all have a future
it won't be found through national pride.
For we are all a speck
in some enormous cosmic eye.

We are men and women of this world.

Give Me Life

Give me life, love and laughter in equal measure.
The devotion of a friendly woman.
Wash away my past and present misdemeanours.
Show me the difference between riches and Fool's
Gold,
there lies the paradox within.

Give me open road, no bother,
with kindness as my guide.
All fear and danger held at bay.
All tears and anguish returned into
the lake from where they came.

Give me life, a journey to be savoured.
My family, friends and loves
raised into a state of Grace.

Let the cards fall where they may.
A life complete with heartfelt songs
and strong emotions.
Just let me write, recite my tempered rhymes,
the bitter and the sweet.
Give me life without the grief.

Well Chosen Words

Well chosen words
roll off the tongue, the gifted few.
A step beyond our searching hearts
one honest rhyme to see us through.

Pen and paper
your tools of trade
a weapon that can bring down tyrants,
make friends and lovers swoon.

The thrust and parry.
Verbs and adjectives
to cut your enemies to size.

Sometimes you travel underground
Avoid the crush of popularity.
Though we know what's on your mind
you blend in with the scenery.

Well chosen words
you take us there.
To never, never tomorrows.
To Kansas, where the wild winds blow
a turn of phrase will bring us home.

Our hearts desire,
a shift in the weather.
Well chosen words
to while away the hours
when there's nothing left to do.

Kid Gloves

Purely on a whim one day.
Thought I'd learn to fight, in a manly way.
Learn the Marquise of Queensbury Rules.
Learn the art of fist-a-cuffs in
a mannered sort of way.

The shuffle of Mohammed Ali.
Or that wiley, wiry oriental chap,
spontaneous combustion,
the sadly missed … Bruce Lee.

A stint at the local gym.
Sparing partners in the ring.
The smell a cornucopia of sweat,
dencorub and tiger balm.
A cavalcade of bruises to the upper skull,
broken noses and ears the shape of cauliflowers.

Soon I chose to work alone
Bringing boxing gear into my home.
The gloves, the shorts and punching bags.
A nautilus and gaffer tape for blistered
swollen fingers.

Sadly, as the days went on
I found my weaknesses were strong.
You see dear reader, I could not stand
The sight of blood.
Although my punches landed well and true.

The biggest hurdle yet to come.
When all was said and all was done,

The Artist's Disease

never having fought for God, Queen and country.
Became the unkindest cut of all.
My soon to be discovered, fragile,
sensitive … glass jaw.

Perhaps I'll take up pottery,
perhaps another story,
Time for hanging up my kid gloves.
Never more a stopping. I'll say farewell to
champeen glory …

Damien Pragnell

Ode To An Aussie Outhouse

Such walls of ironbark and masonite.
To house a modest throne.
A midnight dash with dimming torch,
the door swings back, then loudly shuts,

A modicum of privacy.
The trip you make ... alone.

Pondering the possibilities,
why does that spider nest in here
why is the world so round
as crickets chirp in unison
hidden underground.

The mad dash back to home and bed
the trees cast ghostly shadows.
Come morning when collectors call,
driving by without a word
you sleep so still and sound.

The Great Aussie Outhouse.
An ancient seat of learning,
a symbol of quiet reflection.
Vanishing ... with a modern flush,
around a mighty bend.

The midnight dash, a skip and jump
across the polished floor.
The indoor loo casts no shadows,
no time for soulful contemplation,
someone waits outside the door

The Artist's Disease

dying to get in.

True Believers

As any true Believer knows,
to be truly Born Again
you have to die at least once.

Take it from this former Class Clown,
this College Dunce.

It isn't worth a punt.

Rock and Roll free 'ya! A song you take into the
grave.
Every body"s got a book inside them
but most can't see the written page.

Politicians kid themselves
convincing us their True Believers.
One day they'll be milling around heavens gates,
Saint Peter laughing in their face.

Banished to the other place.

True Believers sail a gentler course.
No need to fear the consequences.
No need to follow Man Made Laws.

A friend once summed it up so well.

True Believers are The Master Race.

Country Woman

I want a country woman.
To sing to me the whole night through.
Songs of love and decency
songs of devotion
songs that all ring true.

I want a country woman
with simple tastes.
Someone to love not just for looks
someone who will stand her ground.

Slim or large doesn't matter much.
I'll know her good intentions.
The conviction of her love.
In return I cannot offer much
in possessions or in cash
yet , all my love within my heart
to see our love come true.

Searching for a country woman
to dance with me when the music plays
a dance of sweet communion
God's plan for both of us.

Heavenly Bodies

A crippled frame.
A mind of crystal clarity.
An electronic eye.
Scanning distant galaxies,
for signs of life.

Written in "A Brief History Of Time."
The story of the universe, seen through
glass, magnified.

Returning to the birth of space.
Lethal gas and swirling dust.
When meteors were tossed asunder.
Molten planets born.

Men with childlike vision.
Who followed eastern stars.
Sailed where there be dragons.
Guided by heavenly bodies,
sparkling brightly in the night.

The worlds beyond the far horizon.
Astronomy, spying on creation, science
or religion,
the answer undecided.

A cosmic spec, our earthly home.
Light years from the possibility,
of neighbours contact.
Are we all alone?
A desperate need to know…

The Artist's Disease

A search for heavenly bodies.
Look no further than your own backyard.
The stars at night are free to observe,
to delight in, to ponder why,
to rediscover long lost dreams.

Teenage Curiosity

Appearing like a Jesus freak,
steel trap mind and lizard smile.
The masses gather at your feet.
Worshipping your silver tongue.

Are you just a teenage curiosity?

The auditoriums and pubs a crush
wherever you appear.
The tattoos and tee shirts bare
your every pose.
You turn the water into beer.

You stand so tall, ashen white
basking in the adulation,
the artificial light,
voice cracked from saying way too much.

Are you just a teenage curiosity
the crowds can't get enough.

The radio thunders with the message.
You could not take the adulation.
Could not live up to your reputation.
Sundays show is cancelled.

Another teenage curiosity takes your place
Dedicates the first song to your memory.

Have you found your long awaited …
immortality…

The Replacements

One hundred thousand hit the sand.
Try in vain to make a stand.
Drifting silently, out to sea.
No crosses mark where they have died.
Their replacements have arrived.

One hundred thousand valentines.
Roses sent to names with no address.
Lovers tired of spoken words,
remembering better times.
The replacements have arrived.

One hundred thousand unemployed.
Walk the weary roads.
Searching for employment,
a place to eat and sleep.
Endless governments send them on a quest so
futile.
Their replacements have arrived.

One hundred thousand scream for life.
In nurseries around the world.
Clutching to their mother's breasts,
reassured they will not be denied.
Their replacements have arrived.

Damien Pragnell

Murderous Complex
An Alibi Gone Wrong

Where were you last night
between the hours of seven and nine?

I was crashed out watching David Attenborough.

Not much of an alibi. It simply will not do!
Was your girlfriend Terri with you?

Yes, she was washing and ironing my work clothes.

Can you explain that bloodstain seeping
through your denim jacket?

Well how on earth did that get there.
I really have no clue.

Think you better come down to the Station
Answer some more questions.

But my girlfriends coming over,
She's going to fix me dinner.

Sorry son, she's baked her last Pavlova.
That was her specialty, wasn't it?

My God what on earth has happened?

Son, she was the victim of a brutal slaying.
Who would do such a despicable act?

The Artist's Disease

Well son, you"re our prime suspect.
Do you mind if we check out the cellar?
I never laid a finger on her
-We will see if that holds up in court.
Yes, by God I can.
Because at the time that is in question,
I was far too busy … chopping up her mother!

Who Will Cry For Watha

Who will cry for Watha.
There is no need for tears.
He has his music and fine words,
to see him through the years.

The grass grew lush and green
Upon the sacred plains.
Watha climbed out of his tee pee
to enjoy the summer rain,
his girlfriend Leslie was not with him,
they had gone their separate ways.

Watha walked the river bank.
Hunting, fishing,
while others gathered berries and sweet corn.
They lived where they belonged, you see.

On star filled nights the ceremonies
had great power.
Blood brothers and sisters all.
Tankashila brought the tribes together
offering a pipe of peace.

Watha carved a saying on a piece of skin.

"Only a fool brings trouble on himself."

While the Shaman cast his spells.

The sun retired slowly.
Oblivious to time.

The Artist's Disease

Yet time is running out,
for us to live this way.

So, who will cry for Watha.
Now content to sit inside his tee pee,
writing on his life.
So, who will cry for Watha.
He's no longer ready made for hire.
Will we be forever known.
As the tribe who gave up paradise.
To wallow in such misery.